EMPHYSEMA HEALTHCARE EDUCATION

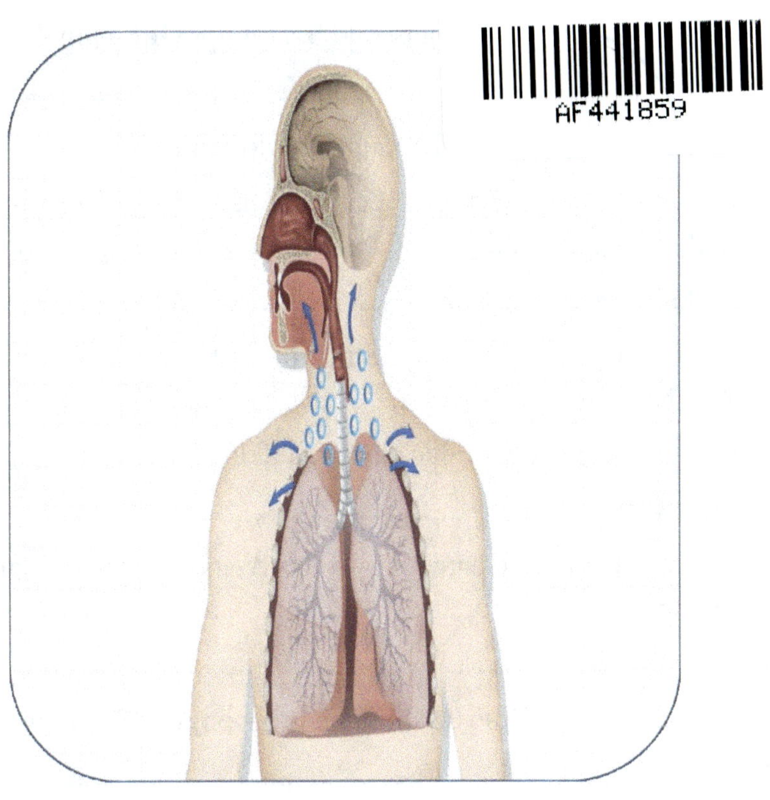

Table Of Contents

<u>**COURSE OVERVIEW**</u>

This comprehensive course is designed to equip healthcare providers, including respiratory therapists, doctors, and nurses, with in-depth knowledge and practical skills to effectively manage and treat patients with emphysema. Emphysema, a type of chronic obstructive pulmonary disease (COPD), requires a multifaceted approach to care that encompasses understanding its pathophysiology, accurately diagnosing the condition, implementing evidence-based treatments, and providing holistic support to patients and caregivers.

<u>**COURSE OBJECTIVE**</u>

By the end of this course, participants will be able to understand the Pathophysiology of Emphysema, Diagnose Emphysema Accurately, Implement Pharmacological Treatments, Apply Non-Pharmacological Interventions, Manage Exacerbations, Promote Long-Term Management and Patient Education, Explore Innovations and Future Direction, Incorporate Nutrition and Lifestyle Modifications, Support Patients and Caregivers. Through achieving these objectives, participants will be well-equipped to deliver high-quality, patient-centered care to individuals with emphysema, improving their health outcomes and quality of life.

<u>**COURSE MATERIALS**</u>

To learn this course, **healthcare providers/ participants** must be provided with materials like a Pen, pencil, notebook, and notepad to better understand and make it easy for them to learn.

INTRODUCTION

Emphysema, a chronic obstructive pulmonary disease (COPD), stands as a significant health challenge for millions worldwide. This condition, characterized by the destruction of the air sacs (alveoli) in the lungs, leads to severe breathing difficulties and a decline in overall respiratory function. For healthcare providers, understanding the intricate details of emphysema is crucial for effective diagnosis, management, and treatment. This book, "Emphysema Unveiled: A Comprehensive Guide for Healthcare Providers," is crafted with the intention of offering a thorough educational resource for respiratory therapists, doctors, and nurses who are at the forefront of patient care.

In the realm of pulmonary diseases, emphysema demands a comprehensive understanding due to its complex nature and multifaceted impact on the human body. The pathophysiology of emphysema involves the gradual destruction of lung tissue, resulting in the loss of elastic recoil, airway collapse, and obstruction during exhalation. This progressive degeneration impairs the ability to breathe effectively, causing chronic shortness of breath, persistent cough, and a diminished capacity for physical activity.

The journey to mastering emphysema care begins with a solid foundation of its clinical presentation and progression. This book delves into the nuances of clinical signs and symptoms, equipping healthcare providers with the knowledge to recognize and diagnose emphysema with precision. From the subtle early indicators to the more pronounced manifestations in advanced stages, each symptom is explored in detail, emphasizing the importance of early detection and intervention.

MODULE ONE

LESSON ONE: UNDERSTANDING EMPHYSEMA

Emphysema is a chronic lung condition that falls under the broader category of chronic obstructive pulmonary disease (COPD). It is characterized by the destruction of the alveoli, the small air sacs in the lungs where the exchange of oxygen and carbon dioxide takes place. This destruction leads to a reduction in the surface area available for gas exchange, causing difficulty in breathing and a decrease in oxygen supply to the body's tissues.

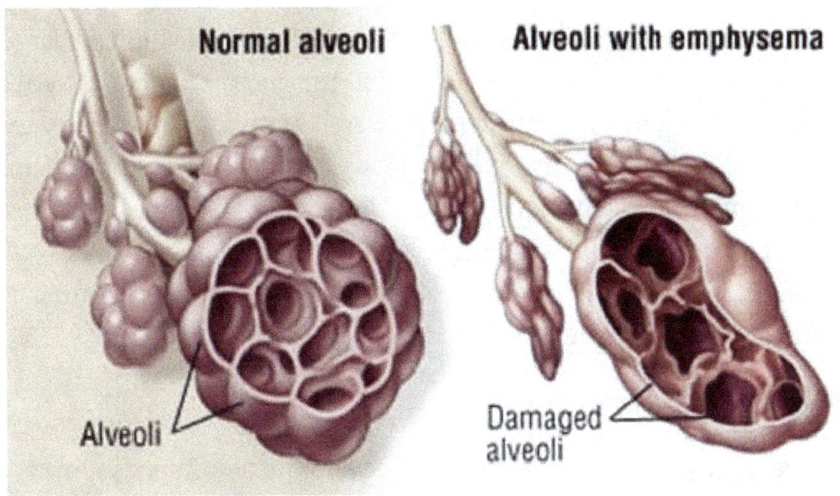

Historical Background and Epidemiology

The term "emphysema" comes from the Greek word "emphysan," meaning "to inflate." The condition was first described in medical literature in the early 19th century, but it wasn't until the 20th century that significant strides were made in understanding its pathophysiology and management. Emphysema primarily affects older adults and is strongly associated with long-term smoking. However, it can also occur in individuals with a genetic predisposition, such as those with alpha-1 antitrypsin deficiency, a hereditary condition that can lead to early-onset emphysema.

Pathophysiology

The primary pathological feature of emphysema is the irreversible destruction of the alveolar walls. This destruction is mainly caused by an imbalance between proteases, enzymes that break down proteins, and antiproteases, which inhibit these enzymes. In healthy lungs, a balance exists between these opposing forces, maintaining the structural integrity of the alveoli. However, in emphysema, this balance is disrupted, leading to excessive protease activity and subsequent alveolar destruction.

The destruction of alveolar walls results in the formation of large, irregular air spaces called bullae, which replace the normal alveolar clusters. This loss of alveolar surface area significantly impairs gas exchange, leading to hypoxemia (low blood oxygen levels) and hypercapnia (elevated blood carbon dioxide levels). The lungs also lose their elastic recoil, which is crucial for maintaining open airways during exhalation. As a result, small airways collapse, leading to airflow obstruction and air trapping.

Risk Factors

Several risk factors contribute to the development of emphysema:

- Smoking: The most significant risk factor, accounting for the majority of emphysema cases. The harmful chemicals in cigarette smoke cause inflammation and damage to lung tissue.
- Genetic Factors: Alpha-1 antitrypsin deficiency is a well-known genetic risk factor. This protein normally protects the lungs from enzyme damage, and its deficiency leads to uncontrolled protease activity.

- Environmental Exposures: Long-term exposure to air pollutants, occupational dust, and chemical fumes can increase the risk of developing emphysema.
- Age: Emphysema is more common in individuals over the age of 40, with the risk increasing with age.
- Gender: Historically, emphysema was more common in men, but the prevalence in women has been rising due to increased smoking rates among women.

Clinical Presentation

The symptoms of emphysema typically develop gradually and worsen over time. Common clinical features include:

- Dyspnea (Shortness of Breath): The hallmark symptom, often starting with exertion and progressing to occur at rest in advanced stages.
- Chronic Cough: A persistent cough, often accompanied by sputum production, is common in patients with a history of smoking.
- Wheezing: A whistling sound during breathing, indicative of airway obstruction.
- Chest Tightness: A feeling of tightness or discomfort in the chest, often exacerbated by physical activity.
- Weight Loss and Muscle Wasting: Advanced emphysema can lead to significant weight loss and muscle wasting due to increased energy expenditure and decreased appetite.

Diagnosis

The diagnosis of emphysema involves a combination of clinical evaluation, pulmonary function tests (PFTs), and imaging studies. Key diagnostic tools include:

- Pulmonary Function Tests (PFTs): Spirometry is the most common PFT used to diagnose emphysema. It measures the amount of air a person can exhale forcefully after taking a deep breath, as well as how quickly they can do so. Emphysema typically shows a reduction in forced expiratory volume in one second (FEV1) and the ratio of FEV1 to forced vital capacity (FVC).

- Imaging Studies: Chest X-rays and computed tomography (CT) scans are essential for visualizing the extent of lung damage. CT scans, in particular, can identify the presence of bullae and other structural abnormalities associated with emphysema.

Management and Prognosis

While emphysema is a progressive and incurable disease, several management strategies can help alleviate symptoms, improve quality of life, and slow disease progression. These include:

- Smoking Cessation: The single most effective intervention to halt disease progression.
- Medications: Bronchodilators, corticosteroids, and other medications can help manage symptoms and reduce exacerbations.
- Pulmonary Rehabilitation: A comprehensive program that includes exercise training, education, and behavioral changes to improve respiratory function and overall health.
- Oxygen Therapy: For patients with severe hypoxemia, supplemental oxygen can improve survival and quality of life.
- Surgical Interventions: In select cases, procedures such as lung volume reduction surgery or lung transplantation may be considered.

The prognosis for emphysema varies depending on the severity of the disease, the patient's overall health, and their ability to adhere to treatment plans. Early diagnosis and proactive management are key to improving outcomes for patients with emphysema.

- How do the structural changes in the lungs associated with emphysema contribute to the clinical symptoms observed in patients?
- What are the primary risk factors for developing emphysema, and how can early intervention help mitigate these risks?

LESSON TWO: CLINICAL SIGNS AND SYMPTOMS OF EMPHYSEMA

Emphysema presents with a range of clinical signs and symptoms that vary in severity depending on the stage of the disease. Recognizing these signs early is crucial for timely diagnosis and intervention, which can significantly improve patient outcomes. In this lesson, we will explore the key clinical features of emphysema, from the subtle initial symptoms to the more pronounced manifestations observed in advanced stages.

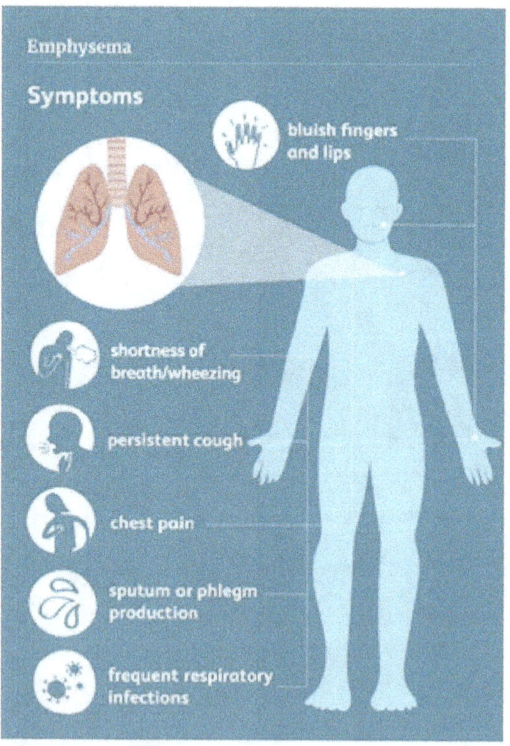

Early Signs and Symptoms

Dyspnea (Shortness of Breath): One of the earliest and most prominent symptoms of emphysema is dyspnea, or shortness of breath. Initially, patients may experience breathlessness during physical exertion, such as climbing stairs or engaging in exercise. As the disease progresses, dyspnea becomes more persistent and can occur even at rest. This symptom is primarily due to the loss of alveolar surface area, which impairs gas exchange and reduces the lungs' capacity to oxygenate the blood.

- Chronic Cough: A chronic cough, often accompanied by sputum production, is another common early symptom of emphysema. This cough is usually more pronounced in the morning and can be mistaken for a smoker's cough. It is a result of chronic inflammation and irritation of the airways caused by smoking or other environmental exposures.
- Wheezing: Wheezing, characterized by a high-pitched whistling sound during breathing, is indicative of airway obstruction. This symptom is often heard during exhalation and can vary in intensity depending on the severity of the obstruction.
- Fatigue: Patients with emphysema often experience fatigue and a general sense of tiredness. This is due to the increased effort required to breathe and the reduced oxygen supply to the body's tissues.

Progressive Symptoms

As emphysema advances, the symptoms become more severe and debilitating. The following are common progressive symptoms:

- Increased Dyspnea: As the disease progresses, shortness of breath becomes more pronounced and persistent. Patients may struggle with daily activities such as walking, dressing, and even talking. The severity of dyspnea is often a key indicator of disease progression.
- Cyanosis: Cyanosis, a bluish discoloration of the skin and mucous membranes, occurs due to low levels of oxygen in the blood. It is most commonly observed in the lips, fingernails,

and earlobes. Cyanosis is a sign of advanced emphysema and indicates significant impairment in gas exchange.

- Barrel Chest: Over time, patients with emphysema may develop a barrel-shaped chest. This physical change results from the overinflation of the lungs and the loss of lung elasticity. The increased anterior-posterior diameter of the chest is a hallmark sign of advanced emphysema.
- Pursed-Lip Breathing: Many patients with emphysema adopt a technique known as pursed-lip breathing. By exhaling through pursed lips, they create back pressure in the airways, helping to keep them open longer and facilitating better air exchange. This technique can alleviate some of the breathlessness associated with emphysema.
- Weight Loss and Muscle Wasting: Advanced emphysema can lead to significant weight loss and muscle wasting, a condition known as cachexia. The increased work of breathing and systemic inflammation contribute to this deterioration in nutritional status and muscle mass.

Exacerbations

Exacerbations, or acute worsening of symptoms, are common in patients with emphysema. These episodes are often triggered by respiratory infections, environmental pollutants, or other stressors. During exacerbations, patients may experience:

- Increased Dyspnea: A sudden worsening of shortness of breath that is more severe than the usual daily variations.
- Increased Sputum Production: An increase in the volume and purulence of sputum, often indicative of a bacterial infection.
- Chest Tightness: A sensation of tightness or discomfort in the chest that can be distressing for patients.
- Increased Cough: A more persistent and severe cough, sometimes accompanied by wheezing.

- Exacerbations can lead to a rapid decline in lung function and overall health, requiring prompt medical intervention. Management of exacerbations typically involves the use of bronchodilators, corticosteroids, antibiotics (if an infection is present), and supplemental oxygen.

Physical Examination Findings

During a physical examination, healthcare providers may observe several signs that are indicative of emphysema. These include:

- Hyperinflation: Increased lung volume and hyperresonance to percussion due to overinflated lungs.
- Decreased Breath Sounds: Diminished breath sounds on auscultation, reflecting the loss of alveolar tissue and reduced airflow.
- Prolonged Expiration: Prolonged expiratory phase during breathing, as patients struggle to exhale air from the lungs.
- Use of Accessory Muscles: Increased use of accessory muscles of respiration, such as the sternocleidomastoid and intercostal muscles, to aid in breathing.

Differential Diagnosis

It is important to differentiate emphysema from other respiratory conditions that present with similar symptoms. Differential diagnoses may include:

- Chronic Bronchitis: Another form of COPD characterized by chronic productive cough and mucus hypersecretion.
- Asthma: A condition with reversible airway obstruction, often with a history of allergic symptoms and episodic wheezing.
- Heart Failure: Can present with dyspnea and cough but is usually associated with other cardiac symptoms and signs.

- Interstitial Lung Disease: A group of disorders characterized by inflammation and fibrosis of the lung interstitium, leading to restrictive lung disease.

Accurate diagnosis requires a comprehensive clinical evaluation, pulmonary function testing, and imaging studies. Understanding the clinical signs and symptoms of emphysema is essential for early diagnosis and effective management. Recognizing the progression of symptoms, identifying exacerbations, and conducting thorough physical examinations are crucial steps in providing optimal care for patients with emphysema.

DISCUSSION QUESTIONS

- What are the key clinical signs and symptoms that healthcare providers should look for when diagnosing emphysema?
- How do imaging techniques, such as chest X-rays and CT scans, aid in the diagnosis and assessment of emphysema?

MODULE TWO

LESSON ONE: PHYSIOLOGICAL IMPACTS OF EMPHYSEMA

Emphysema exerts profound effects on the physiological functioning of the lungs and the overall respiratory system. This lesson will explore the various physiological changes that occur in emphysema, providing a detailed understanding of how the disease impairs lung function and affects the body's ability to oxygenate the blood and expel carbon dioxide.

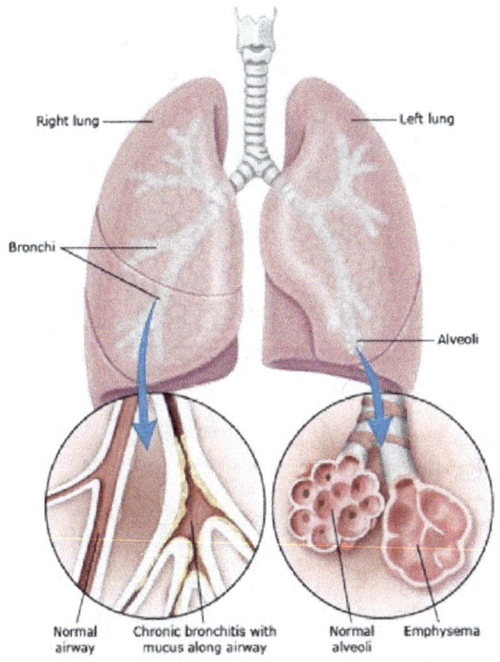

Alveolar Destruction and Loss of Elastic Recoil

The hallmark of emphysema is the destruction of the alveolar walls, leading to the formation of large air spaces known as bullae. This destruction results from an imbalance between proteases and antiproteases in the lungs, often exacerbated by smoking or genetic factors such as alpha-1 antitrypsin deficiency.

The loss of alveolar walls reduces the surface area available for gas exchange, impairing the lungs' ability to oxygenate the blood and remove carbon dioxide. Additionally, the destruction of the alveolar walls leads to a loss of elastic recoil, which is crucial for maintaining open airways during exhalation. The decreased elastic recoil results in airway collapse, particularly during forced exhalation, leading to airflow obstruction and air trapping.

Airflow Obstruction and Air Trapping

Airflow obstruction in emphysema is primarily caused by the collapse of small airways during exhalation. The loss of elastic recoil and the structural changes in the airways contribute to this phenomenon. As a result, patients experience difficulty in exhaling air completely, leading to air trapping and hyperinflation of the lungs.

Hyperinflation increases the work of breathing, as the respiratory muscles must exert more effort to overcome the increased lung volume and resistance to airflow. This increased effort contributes to the sensation of dyspnea, or shortness of breath, which is a primary symptom of emphysema.

Impaired Gas Exchange

The destruction of the alveolar-capillary membrane in emphysema significantly impairs gas exchange. The reduction in alveolar surface area decreases the efficiency of oxygen uptake and carbon dioxide elimination. This impairment leads to hypoxemia (low blood oxygen levels) and hypercapnia (elevated blood carbon dioxide levels).

Hypoxemia occurs because the reduced alveolar surface area limits the amount of oxygen that can diffuse into the blood. Hypercapnia results from the decreased ability to eliminate carbon dioxide, which accumulates in the blood. These gas exchange abnormalities can lead to a range of systemic effects, including fatigue, confusion, and decreased exercise tolerance.

V/Q Mismatch

Ventilation-perfusion (V/Q) mismatch is a key feature of emphysema. In healthy lungs, ventilation (airflow) and perfusion (blood flow) are well-matched, ensuring efficient gas exchange. However, in emphysema, the destruction of alveolar tissue and the presence of bullae disrupt this balance.

Areas of the lung that are well-ventilated may have reduced blood flow due to capillary destruction, while areas with adequate blood flow may be poorly ventilated due to airway obstruction and air trapping. This mismatch leads to inefficient gas exchange, contributing to hypoxemia and hypercapnia.

Pulmonary Hypertension

Pulmonary hypertension, or elevated blood pressure in the pulmonary arteries, can develop as a complication of emphysema. The destruction of the alveolar-capillary membrane and the resulting hypoxemia lead to vasoconstriction of the pulmonary arteries. Over time, this increased resistance to blood flow can cause the right side of the heart to work harder, leading to right ventricular hypertrophy and eventually right-sided heart failure (cor pulmonale).

Pulmonary hypertension exacerbates the symptoms of emphysema, increasing dyspnea and reducing exercise tolerance. It also complicates the management of the disease and is associated with a poorer prognosis.

Systemic Effects

Emphysema not only affects the lungs but also has systemic consequences. The chronic hypoxemia and hypercapnia associated with the disease can lead to systemic inflammation and metabolic changes. Patients with emphysema are at increased risk for conditions such as cardiovascular disease, osteoporosis, and skeletal muscle dysfunction.

Systemic inflammation in emphysema is driven by the release of inflammatory mediators from the lungs, which can affect other organs and tissues. This inflammation contributes to the development of comorbid conditions and impacts the overall health and well-being of patients.

The physiological impacts of emphysema are multifaceted and involve complex interactions between alveolar destruction, airflow obstruction, impaired gas exchange, and systemic effects. Understanding these physiological changes is essential for developing effective treatment strategies and providing comprehensive care for patients with emphysema.

DISCUSSION QUESTIONS

- How do bronchodilators and corticosteroids work to alleviate the symptoms of emphysema, and what are their potential side effects?
- What are the emerging pharmacological treatments for emphysema, and how do they differ from traditional therapies?

LESSON TWO: RADIOGRAPHIC FEATURES; IDENTIFYING EMPHYSEMA ON X-RAYS

Radiographic imaging plays a crucial role in the diagnosis and management of emphysema. Chest X-rays and computed tomography (CT) scans provide valuable insights into the structural changes and extent of lung damage associated with the disease. This lesson will explore the key radiographic features of emphysema and offer guidance on interpreting these findings in clinical practice.

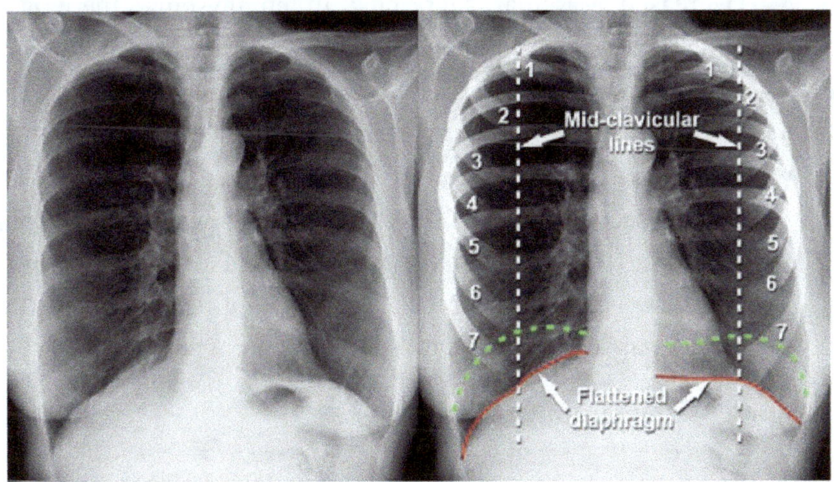

Chest X-rays

Chest X-rays are a common and readily available imaging modality used to evaluate patients with suspected emphysema. While they may not be as detailed as CT scans, X-rays can provide important clues to the presence and severity of emphysema.

- Hyperinflation: One of the most prominent features of emphysema on a chest X-ray is hyperinflation of the lungs. This is characterized by an increased lung volume, which can be observed as an expanded rib cage and a flattened diaphragm. The increased anterior-posterior diameter of the chest is often referred to as a "barrel chest" appearance.

- Flattened Diaphragm: The diaphragm, the primary muscle of respiration, becomes flattened and less domed in shape due to lung hyperinflation. This flattening is a result of the increased lung volume and the loss of elastic recoil.

- Increased Retrosternal Air Space: The space behind the sternum (retrosternal air space) is often increased in patients with emphysema. This finding is best appreciated on a lateral chest X-ray and is indicative of lung hyperinflation.

- Decreased Vascular Markings: In emphysema, there is a reduction in the number and prominence of pulmonary vascular markings. This is due to the destruction of the alveolar-capillary network and the loss of lung tissue.

- Bullae and Blebs: Large air-filled spaces, known as bullae, can be seen on chest X-rays in patients with emphysema. These bullae result from the destruction of alveolar walls and can vary in size and number. Smaller air-filled spaces, called blebs, may also be present.

Computed Tomography (CT) Scans

CT scans provide a more detailed and accurate assessment of the structural changes in the lungs associated with emphysema. They are particularly useful for identifying the presence and extent of bullae and for assessing the distribution of emphysematous changes.

- Centrilobular Emphysema: This is the most common type of emphysema and is typically associated with smoking. It predominantly affects the upper lobes of the lungs and is characterized by the destruction of the central portions of the secondary pulmonary lobules. On CT scans, centrilobular emphysema appears as small, round areas of low attenuation with well-defined borders.

- Panlobular Emphysema: Panlobular emphysema is often associated with alpha-1 antitrypsin deficiency and affects the entire secondary pulmonary lobule uniformly. It is usually more diffuse and involves the lower lobes of the lungs. On CT scans, panlobular emphysema appears as a diffuse decrease in lung attenuation without a clear demarcation between affected and normal areas.

- Paraseptal Emphysema: This type of emphysema affects the distal parts of the secondary pulmonary lobules, particularly the subpleural regions and areas adjacent to the interlobular septa. On CT scans, paraseptal emphysema appears as areas of low attenuation along the lung periphery and interlobular septa.

- Bullae and Blebs: CT scans provide a clear and detailed visualization of bullae and blebs. Bullae are large air-filled spaces that can occupy significant portions of the lung and may cause compression of adjacent lung tissue. Blebs are smaller air-filled spaces that are usually located near the lung surface.

- Air Trapping: Air trapping, a common feature of emphysema, can be assessed using expiratory CT scans. During expiration, areas of the lung affected by emphysema may retain air and appear as regions of low attenuation. This finding helps differentiate emphysema from other lung conditions.

Differential Diagnosis

When interpreting radiographic findings, it is important to differentiate emphysema from other conditions that may present with similar imaging features. Differential diagnoses may include:

- Chronic Bronchitis: Often presents with increased bronchial markings and airway wall thickening, but without the hyperinflation and bullae characteristic of emphysema.

- Interstitial Lung Disease: Characterized by diffuse interstitial infiltrates, reticular or nodular patterns, and honeycombing in advanced stages.
- Asthma: May show hyperinflation and increased bronchial markings during exacerbations, but typically lacks the structural changes seen in emphysema.
- Pneumothorax: The presence of air in the pleural space can cause lung collapse and may mimic the appearance of bullae on imaging studies.

Radiographic imaging is an essential tool in the diagnosis and management of emphysema. Chest X-rays and CT scans provide valuable insights into the structural changes and extent of lung damage associated with the disease. By understanding the key radiographic features of emphysema and differentiating it from other conditions, healthcare providers can make accurate diagnoses and develop effective treatment plans.

DISCUSSION QUESTIONS

- How does pulmonary rehabilitation benefit patients with emphysema, and what are the key components of an effective rehabilitation program?
- What surgical options are available for severe emphysema, and what are the criteria for considering these interventions?

MODULE THREE

LESSON ONE: TREATMENT STRATEGIES; FROM MEDICATIONS TO REHABILITATION

Effective management of emphysema requires a comprehensive approach that addresses the underlying pathophysiology, alleviates symptoms, and improves overall quality of life. This lesson will explore the various treatment strategies for emphysema, including pharmacological interventions, pulmonary rehabilitation, and surgical options.

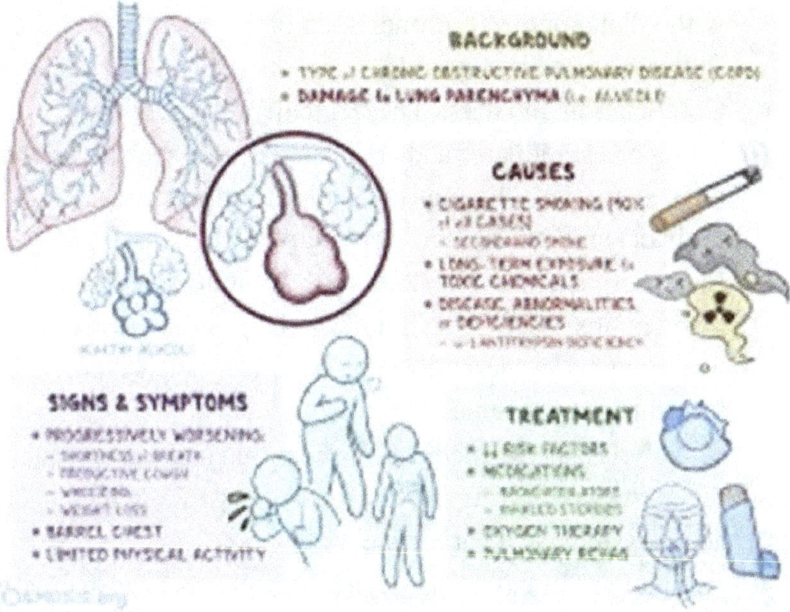

Pharmacological Interventions

Medications play a crucial role in the management of emphysema, helping to relieve symptoms, reduce exacerbations, and improve lung function. The following are key pharmacological treatments used in the management of emphysema:

- Bronchodilators: These medications help relax the muscles around the airways, making it easier to breathe. They are typically administered via inhalers or nebulizers and can be short-acting (for quick relief) or long-acting (for maintenance therapy). Common bronchodilators include:
  - ✓ Short-acting beta-agonists (SABAs), such as albuterol.
  - ✓ Long-acting beta-agonists (LABAs), such as salmeterol and formoterol.
  - ✓ Anticholinergics, such as ipratropium (short-acting) and tiotropium (long-acting).
- Inhaled Corticosteroids (ICS): These medications help reduce inflammation in the airways, decreasing the frequency and severity of exacerbations. They are often used in combination with long-acting bronchodilators. Examples include fluticasone and budesonide.
- Combination Inhalers: These inhalers contain both a long-acting bronchodilator and an inhaled corticosteroid, providing dual benefits. Examples include fluticasone/salmeterol (Advair) and budesonide/formoterol (Symbicort).
- Phosphodiesterase-4 (PDE-4) Inhibitors: These oral medications, such as roflumilast, help reduce inflammation and prevent exacerbations in patients with severe COPD, including emphysema.
- Mucolytics: These medications help thin and loosen mucus in the airways, making it easier to clear. Examples include acetylcysteine and carbocisteine.
- Antibiotics: In cases of bacterial infections or exacerbations triggered by infections, antibiotics may be prescribed to treat the underlying infection and prevent further complications.

Pulmonary Rehabilitation

Pulmonary rehabilitation is a comprehensive program designed to improve the physical and emotional well-being of patients with chronic lung diseases, including emphysema. The components of pulmonary rehabilitation include:

- Exercise Training: A tailored exercise program helps improve cardiovascular fitness, muscle strength, and endurance. Regular physical activity can reduce dyspnea and enhance overall quality of life.
- Education: Patients receive education on disease management, proper use of medications and inhalers, breathing techniques, and strategies to cope with the symptoms of emphysema.
- Nutritional Support: Nutritional counseling helps address weight loss and muscle wasting, ensuring patients receive adequate nutrition to maintain muscle mass and energy levels.
- Psychosocial Support: Counseling and support groups help patients manage the emotional challenges associated with emphysema, such as anxiety and depression.
- Smoking Cessation: Smoking cessation is a critical component of pulmonary rehabilitation, as continued smoking can accelerate the progression of emphysema and diminish the effectiveness of treatments.

Oxygen Therapy

Oxygen therapy is prescribed for patients with emphysema who have significant hypoxemia (low blood oxygen levels). Long-term oxygen therapy can improve survival, relieve dyspnea, and enhance overall quality of life. Oxygen can be delivered via nasal cannula, face mask, or portable oxygen concentrators, allowing patients to maintain mobility and independence.

Surgical Interventions

In select cases, surgical interventions may be considered for patients with severe emphysema who do not respond adequately to medical treatment. Surgical options include:

- Lung Volume Reduction Surgery (LVRS): This procedure involves the removal of damaged, hyperinflated lung tissue to improve the function of the remaining healthy lung. LVRS can enhance lung mechanics, reduce dyspnea, and improve exercise capacity.
- Bullectomy: This surgery involves the removal of large bullae that compress healthy lung tissue and impair lung function. Bullectomy can improve breathing and reduce symptoms in patients with significant bullae.
- Lung Transplantation: In cases of end-stage emphysema, lung transplantation may be considered. This procedure involves replacing the diseased lungs with healthy donor lungs. Lung transplantation can significantly improve quality of life and survival in carefully selected patients.

The management of emphysema requires a multifaceted approach that includes pharmacological treatments, pulmonary rehabilitation, oxygen therapy, and, in some cases, surgical interventions. By combining these strategies, healthcare providers can effectively manage symptoms, reduce exacerbations, and improve the overall quality of life for patients with emphysema.

DISCUSSION QUESTIONS

- What are the common triggers for exacerbations in emphysema, and how can patients and healthcare providers work to prevent them?
- Discussion Question 2: How should an acute exacerbation of emphysema be managed in a clinical setting, and what are the goals of treatment during these episodes?

LESSON TWO: PATIENT EDUCATION AND SELF-MANAGEMENT

Patient education and self-management are essential components of the long-term care of emphysema. Empowering patients with the knowledge and skills to manage their condition can lead to better health outcomes, improved quality of life, and reduced healthcare utilization. This lesson will explore the key aspects of patient education and self-management in emphysema care.

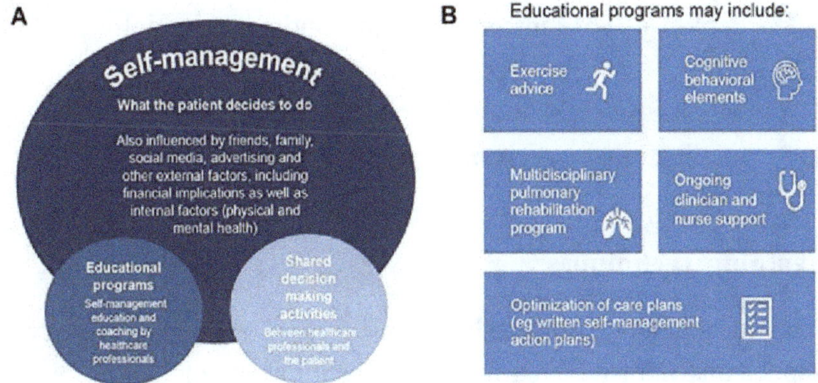

Understanding the Disease

Educating patients about the nature of emphysema is the first step in effective self-management. Patients should understand:

- Pathophysiology: Emphysema is a chronic, progressive lung disease characterized by the destruction of alveolar tissue, leading to airflow obstruction and impaired gas exchange.
- Symptoms: Common symptoms include dyspnea, chronic cough, wheezing, and fatigue. Recognizing early signs of exacerbations is crucial for prompt intervention.
- Risk Factors: Smoking is the primary risk factor for emphysema. Other risk factors include exposure to

environmental pollutants, respiratory infections, and genetic factors such as alpha-1 antitrypsin deficiency.

Medication Adherence

Adherence to prescribed medications is vital for managing symptoms and preventing exacerbations. Patients should be educated on:

- Medication Types: Understanding the different types of medications, including bronchodilators, inhaled corticosteroids, and combination inhalers.
- Proper Inhaler Technique: Demonstrating and practicing the correct use of inhalers to ensure optimal drug delivery to the lungs.
- Medication Schedules: Emphasizing the importance of taking medications as prescribed, including the timing and frequency of doses.

Breathing Techniques

Teaching patients effective breathing techniques can help alleviate dyspnea and improve lung function. Techniques include:

- Pursed-Lip Breathing: Inhaling through the nose and exhaling slowly through pursed lips can help reduce air trapping and improve ventilation.
- Diaphragmatic Breathing: Encouraging deep, diaphragmatic breathing to enhance lung expansion and reduce the work of breathing.

Smoking Cessation

Smoking cessation is the most important intervention for patients with emphysema. Providing support and resources for quitting smoking is essential, including:

- Counseling: Offering individual or group counseling to address the psychological aspects of nicotine addiction.

- Medications: Prescribing nicotine replacement therapy (NRT), bupropion, or varenicline to aid in smoking cessation.
- Support Groups: Connecting patients with support groups and smoking cessation programs for ongoing encouragement and accountability.

Lifestyle Modifications

Encouraging healthy lifestyle choices can improve overall well-being and manage emphysema symptoms. Recommendations include:

- Regular Exercise: Engaging in regular physical activity to improve cardiovascular fitness, muscle strength, and endurance.
- Balanced Diet: Maintaining a nutritious diet to support overall health and prevent weight loss and muscle wasting.
- Hydration: Staying well-hydrated to help thin mucus and facilitate its clearance from the airways.

Recognizing and Managing Exacerbations

Educating patients on how to recognize and manage exacerbations is crucial for preventing complications. Key points include:

- Early Signs: Identifying early signs of exacerbations, such as increased dyspnea, changes in sputum color or volume, and increased cough.
- Action Plan: Developing a personalized action plan for managing exacerbations, including when to use rescue medications and when to seek medical attention.
- Preventive Measures: Implementing preventive measures, such as avoiding respiratory infections, using appropriate vaccinations (e.g., influenza and pneumococcal vaccines), and minimizing exposure to environmental triggers.

Emotional and Psychological Support

Living with emphysema can be challenging, and patients may experience anxiety, depression, and social isolation. Providing emotional and psychological support is essential, including:

- Counseling Services: Referring patients to mental health professionals for individual or group counseling.
- Support Groups: Encouraging participation in support groups for patients with chronic lung diseases to share experiences and coping strategies.
- Stress Management: Teaching stress management techniques, such as relaxation exercises, mindfulness, and deep breathing.

Patient education and self-management are integral to the long-term care of emphysema. By equipping patients with the knowledge and skills to manage their condition, healthcare providers can help improve health outcomes, enhance quality of life, and reduce healthcare utilization.

DISCUSSION QUESTIONS

- What strategies can be implemented to improve adherence to long-term management plans for emphysema patients?
- How can patient education programs enhance self-management skills and overall outcomes for individuals with emphysema?

LESSON ONE: FUTURE DIRECTIONS AND ADVANCEMENTS IN EMPHYSEMA TREATMENT

Advances in Pharmacological Treatments

Research into new pharmacological treatments for emphysema is ongoing, with several promising avenues being explored:

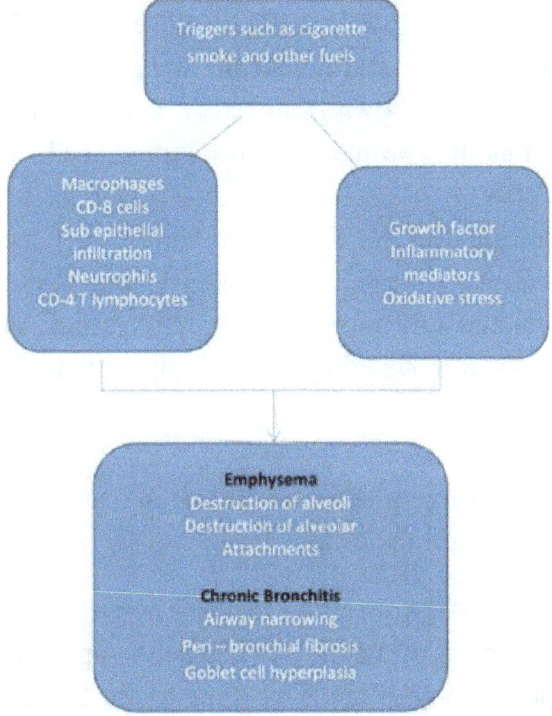

- New Bronchodilators: The development of novel bronchodilators that target different pathways and receptors may provide more effective symptom relief and improved lung function.

- Anti-Inflammatory Agents: Investigating new anti-inflammatory agents that can more specifically target the inflammatory processes involved in emphysema, potentially reducing side effects compared to current corticosteroids.
- Antioxidant Therapies: Exploring the role of oxidative stress in emphysema and the potential benefits of antioxidant therapies to protect lung tissue from damage.

Regenerative Medicine and Stem Cell Therapy

Regenerative medicine and stem cell therapy hold great promise for the treatment of emphysema:

- Stem Cell Therapy: Investigating the potential of stem cell therapy to repair and regenerate damaged lung tissue. Early studies have shown that stem cells may help reduce inflammation, promote tissue repair, and improve lung function.
- Tissue Engineering: Exploring the use of tissue engineering techniques to create bioengineered lung tissue that can be transplanted into patients with emphysema. This approach aims to restore lung function and improve quality of life.

Gene Therapy

Gene therapy is an emerging area of research that holds potential for treating emphysema at the genetic level:

- Alpha-1 Antitrypsin (AAT) Gene Therapy: For patients with alpha-1 antitrypsin deficiency, gene therapy aims to deliver a functional copy of the AAT gene to the liver, allowing it to produce normal levels of the protein and prevent further lung damage.
- Genetic Modulation: Investigating techniques to modulate the expression of genes involved in the pathogenesis of

emphysema, potentially slowing disease progression and improving lung function.

Advances in Surgical Techniques

Innovations in surgical techniques are providing new options for patients with advanced emphysema:

- Minimally Invasive Lung Volume Reduction Surgery (LVRS): Developing less invasive approaches to LVRS, such as bronchoscopic lung volume reduction using endobronchial valves or coils, which can achieve similar benefits with reduced surgical risks and shorter recovery times.
- Improved Transplantation Techniques: Advancing lung transplantation techniques to improve outcomes, reduce complications, and extend the longevity of transplanted lungs.

Personalized Medicine

Personalized medicine, which tailors treatment to the individual characteristics of each patient, is becoming increasingly important in emphysema care:

- Biomarkers: Identifying biomarkers that can predict disease progression, response to treatment, and risk of exacerbations, allowing for more personalized and targeted therapies.
- Genetic Profiling: Using genetic profiling to identify patients who may benefit from specific treatments, such as those with alpha-1 antitrypsin deficiency or other genetic predispositions.

Digital Health and Telemedicine

The integration of digital health technologies and telemedicine is transforming the management of emphysema:

- Remote Monitoring: Implementing remote monitoring devices to track patients' lung function, symptoms, and medication adherence in real-time, allowing for early intervention and personalized care.

- Telemedicine: Expanding the use of telemedicine to provide convenient and accessible healthcare services, including virtual consultations, remote pulmonary rehabilitation, and digital support groups.

The future of emphysema treatment is promising, with ongoing research and advancements offering new hope for patients. From novel pharmacological treatments and regenerative medicine to personalized medicine and digital health, these innovations have the potential to transform the care of emphysema and improve outcomes for patients worldwide. By staying at the forefront of research and embracing emerging therapies, healthcare providers can continue to advance the field and enhance the quality of life for those living with emphysema.

DISCUSSION QUESTIONS

- What are the most promising advancements in emphysema treatment currently being researched, and how might they impact future patient care?
- How can healthcare providers stay informed about emerging therapies and integrate new treatments into their practice effectively?

MODULE FIVE

LESSON ONE: THE ROLE OF NUTRITION IN EMPHYSEMA MANAGEMENT

Nutrition plays a pivotal role in the management of emphysema, impacting everything from immune function and inflammation to muscle strength and overall energy levels. This lesson will explore how dietary choices can influence the progression and symptoms of emphysema, offering practical advice for patients and healthcare providers.

Importance of Nutrition in Emphysema

Proper nutrition is essential for maintaining overall health and managing the symptoms of emphysema. Poor nutritional status can exacerbate the condition, leading to decreased muscle strength, reduced respiratory function, and increased susceptibility to infections.

- Energy Balance: Emphysema patients often have an increased metabolic rate due to the effort required for breathing. Ensuring adequate caloric intake is crucial to prevent weight loss and muscle wasting.

- Protein Intake: Protein is vital for maintaining muscle mass and supporting the immune system. Patients with emphysema should consume sufficient protein to offset the muscle breakdown that can occur with chronic illness.

- Micronutrients: Vitamins and minerals play a critical role in lung health and immune function. Antioxidants, such as vitamins C and E, can help combat oxidative stress and inflammation.

Nutritional Recommendations

- Caloric Needs: Patients with emphysema typically need a higher caloric intake to meet their increased energy demands. A balanced diet with an appropriate mix of carbohydrates, fats, and proteins is essential.

- High-Protein Diet: Emphasize lean protein sources such as poultry, fish, legumes, and low-fat dairy products. Protein supplements may be beneficial for those who struggle to meet their needs through diet alone.

- Healthy Fats: Include sources of healthy fats, such as avocados, nuts, seeds, and olive oil, to provide sustained energy and support cellular health.

- Antioxidant-Rich Foods: Incorporate plenty of fruits and vegetables that are high in antioxidants to help reduce inflammation. Examples include berries, citrus fruits, leafy greens, and bell peppers.

- Hydration: Staying well-hydrated helps to thin mucus, making it easier to clear from the airways. Aim for at least eight glasses of water per day, and avoid dehydrating beverages like caffeinated drinks and alcohol.

Special Considerations

- Eating Strategies: Eating smaller, more frequent meals can help prevent feelings of fullness that may exacerbate breathing difficulties. Patients should avoid large meals and foods that can cause bloating, such as carbonated drinks and cruciferous vegetables.
- Supplements: In some cases, supplements may be necessary to address specific nutritional deficiencies. Omega-3 fatty acids, vitamin D, and calcium are commonly recommended supplements for patients with emphysema.
- Professional Guidance: Working with a registered dietitian can help patients develop a personalized nutrition plan that meets their specific needs and preferences.

Nutrition is a critical component of emphysema management, influencing not only physical health but also the ability to cope with the disease's demands. By adopting a balanced diet rich in essential nutrients and following tailored dietary advice, patients can improve their quality of life and enhance their overall health.

DISCUSSION QUESTIONS

- How can specific dietary changes improve lung function and overall health in patients with emphysema?
- What are the potential challenges that emphysema patients might face in maintaining a nutritious diet, and how can healthcare providers help overcome these challenges

MODULE SIX

LESSON ONE: LIFESTYLE FACTORS AND ENVIRONMENTAL MODIFICATIONS IN EMPHYSEMA MANAGEMENT

Lifestyle factors and environmental modifications play significant roles in the management of emphysema. This lesson will explore how adjustments in daily activities, exercise routines, and living environments can help mitigate symptoms and improve the overall well-being of patients with emphysema.

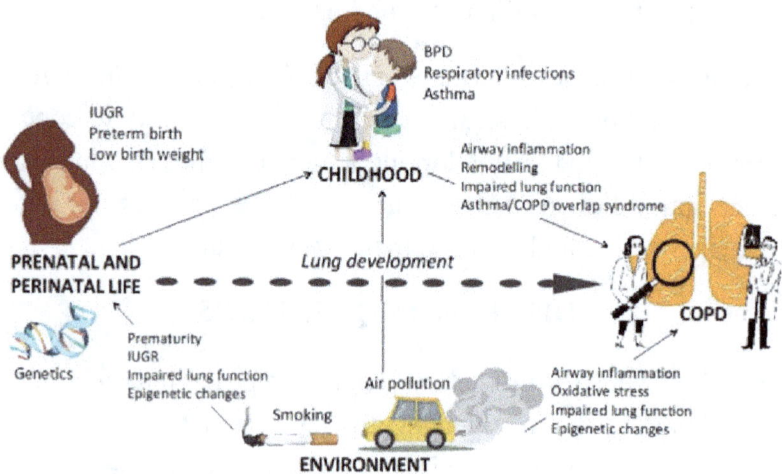

The Role of Exercise

Regular physical activity is essential for maintaining muscle strength, cardiovascular health, and overall stamina in patients with emphysema. Exercise can help reduce breathlessness, improve mood, and enhance the quality of life.

- Aerobic Exercise: Activities such as walking, cycling, and swimming can improve cardiovascular fitness and help manage weight. Patients should aim for at least 150 minutes of moderate-intensity aerobic exercise per week.

- Strength Training: Building muscle strength through resistance exercises, such as weightlifting or using resistance bands, can enhance respiratory muscle function and overall physical endurance. Strength training should be done at least twice a week.
- Breathing Exercises: Techniques such as pursed-lip breathing and diaphragmatic breathing can help improve ventilation and reduce dyspnea during physical activity.
- Customized Exercise Programs: Working with a pulmonary rehabilitation specialist can help patients develop a tailored exercise program that takes into account their specific limitations and goals.

ENVIRONMENTAL MODIFICATIONS

Creating a conducive living environment can significantly impact the management of emphysema. Modifications should aim to reduce exposure to irritants, improve air quality, and facilitate easier breathing.

1. **Indoor Air Quality:**
   - Air Purifiers: Using air purifiers with HEPA filters can help remove airborne particles, allergens, and pollutants from the home environment.
   - Humidity Control: Maintaining optimal humidity levels (30-50%) can help reduce respiratory irritation. Dehumidifiers and humidifiers can be used as needed to achieve this balance.
   - Ventilation: Ensuring good ventilation by regularly opening windows or using exhaust fans can help reduce indoor air pollution.
2. **Avoiding Irritants:**
   - Smoke-Free Environment: Ensuring that the living space is free from tobacco smoke is crucial. This includes avoiding

secondhand smoke and other pollutants such as fumes from cooking, cleaning products, and industrial emissions.

- Chemical-Free Cleaning: Using non-toxic, fragrance-free cleaning products can help reduce exposure to irritants that can exacerbate emphysema symptoms.

3. **Ergonomic Adjustments:**

- Furniture Arrangement: Arranging furniture to minimize the need for excessive movement or bending can help conserve energy and reduce breathlessness.
- Accessibility: Making modifications to improve accessibility, such as installing grab bars in the bathroom, using raised toilet seats, and ensuring that frequently used items are within easy reach, can help patients maintain independence and safety.

4. **Stress Management**

Living with emphysema can be stressful, and managing stress is an important aspect of care. Chronic stress can exacerbate symptoms and impact overall health.

- Relaxation Techniques: Practices such as yoga, meditation, and progressive muscle relaxation can help reduce stress and improve emotional well-being.
- Mindfulness: Mindfulness techniques can help patients stay focused on the present moment, reducing anxiety and improving their ability to cope with the challenges of emphysema.
- Support Systems: Building a strong support network, including family, friends, and support groups, can provide emotional support and practical assistance.

Adopting healthy lifestyle practices and making environmental modifications are crucial steps in managing emphysema effectively. By incorporating regular exercise, optimizing indoor air quality, avoiding irritants, and managing stress, patients can improve their quality of life and better manage the symptoms of emphysema.

DISCUSSION QUESTIONS

- What are the most effective environmental modifications that can help reduce symptoms and improve the quality of life for patients with emphysema?
- How can regular exercise benefit patients with emphysema, and what types of exercises are most recommended?

MODULE SEVEN

LESSON ONE: PATIENT AND CAREGIVER SUPPORT IN EMPHYSEMA MANAGEMENT

Managing emphysema can be challenging not only for patients but also for their caregivers. Providing comprehensive support for both groups is essential for effective disease management and improved quality of life. This lesson will delve into strategies and resources available to support patients and caregivers in navigating the complexities of emphysema.

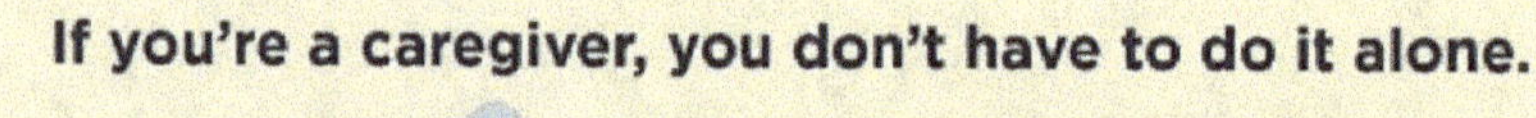

Understanding the Emotional Impact

Living with emphysema can take a toll on emotional well-being, leading to feelings of anxiety, depression, and social isolation. Recognizing and addressing these emotional challenges is crucial for overall health.

- Emotional Well-being of Patients: Patients may experience frustration, sadness, and anxiety about their condition. It's important to acknowledge these feelings and seek professional help when needed.
- Caregiver Stress: Caregivers often face significant stress and burnout from the demands of providing constant care.

Addressing caregiver well-being is essential to sustain their ability to provide effective support.

Building a Support Network

A strong support network can significantly improve the experience of living with emphysema. This network includes healthcare providers, family, friends, and support groups.

- Healthcare Team: Regular communication with healthcare providers, including doctors, respiratory therapists, and nutritionists, ensures that patients receive comprehensive and coordinated care.
- Family and Friends: Engaging family and friends in the care process can provide emotional support, practical assistance, and a sense of community.
- Support Groups: Joining support groups, either in-person or online, allows patients and caregivers to connect with others facing similar challenges, share experiences, and receive encouragement.

Education and Training

Educating patients and caregivers about emphysema is crucial for effective disease management. Understanding the condition, treatment options, and self-management strategies empowers them to make informed decisions.

- Patient Education: Providing detailed information about emphysema, including its symptoms, progression, and treatment options, helps patients understand their condition and take an active role in their care.
- Caregiver Training: Caregivers should receive training on how to assist with daily activities, manage medications, and respond to emergencies. This training can be provided by healthcare professionals or through specialized programs.

Practical Support Strategies

Implementing practical support strategies can help patients manage their symptoms and maintain independence while reducing caregiver burden.

- Medication Management: Using pill organizers, setting reminders, and keeping a medication diary can help ensure that patients take their medications as prescribed.
- Activity Modification: Adapting daily activities to conserve energy and reduce breathlessness can enhance quality of life. This may include using assistive devices, simplifying tasks, and pacing activities.
- Emergency Preparedness: Developing an emergency plan that includes a list of medications, contact information for healthcare providers, and instructions for managing acute exacerbations is essential.

Financial and Legal Considerations

Managing the financial and legal aspects of chronic illness can alleviate stress and ensure that patients and caregivers are prepared for future needs.

- Financial Planning: Understanding insurance coverage, exploring financial assistance programs, and planning for long-term care costs can help manage the financial burden of emphysema.
- Legal Considerations: Preparing legal documents such as advance directives, power of attorney, and living wills ensures that patients' wishes are respected and that caregivers have the authority to make decisions when necessary.

Utilizing Technology

Technology can play a significant role in supporting patients and caregivers by providing tools for communication, monitoring, and education.

- Telemedicine: Virtual consultations with healthcare providers can offer convenient access to medical advice and follow-up care, reducing the need for frequent in-person visits.
- Health Apps: Mobile apps can help patients track symptoms, monitor medication adherence, and access educational resources.
- Online Communities: Participating in online forums and social media groups dedicated to emphysema can provide additional support and information.

Supporting patients and caregivers in the management of emphysema involves addressing emotional, educational, practical, financial, and technological needs. By building a robust support network, providing comprehensive education, implementing practical strategies, and utilizing technology, patients and caregivers can navigate the challenges of emphysema more effectively. Ensuring that both patients and caregivers receive the support they need can significantly improve their quality of life and enhance the overall management of the condition. This holistic approach emphasizes the importance of considering the well-being of both patients and those who care for them, fostering a collaborative and compassionate environment for managing emphysema.

DISCUSSION QUESTIONS

- What are the key elements of an effective support network for emphysema patients, and how can caregivers be better supported in their roles?

- How can technology, such as telemedicine and health apps, improve the management of emphysema for both patients and caregivers?

CONCLUSION

Emphysema, a progressive and debilitating lung disease, requires a multifaceted approach for effective management. This comprehensive guide has delved into the myriad aspects of emphysema care, from understanding its pathophysiology and risk factors to exploring advanced treatment options and supportive care strategies. The importance of recognizing the structural changes and risk factors that contribute to emphysema is crucial for early diagnosis and intervention. Awareness of these factors can help mitigate the disease's progression and improve patient outcomes.

Addressing emphysema effectively requires a multifaceted approach that combines medical treatments, lifestyle changes, and ongoing support. Early diagnosis and intervention can slow the progression of the disease and improve patient outcomes. Research and innovation continue to play a pivotal role in discovering new treatments and enhancing the quality of care for emphysema patients. Healthcare providers must remain vigilant and proactive in managing emphysema, focusing on individualized care plans that address the unique needs of each patient. Patients and caregivers should be encouraged to engage actively in the care process, utilizing available resources and support networks.

While emphysema presents significant challenges, comprehensive care and a holistic approach can make a substantial difference in the lives of those affected. By continuing to advance our understanding of the disease and improving our management strategies, we can offer hope and better quality of life to individuals living with emphysema.

REFERENCES

- Barnes, P.J. (2008). *The role of inflammation and anti-inflammatory treatment in COPD. European Respiratory Journal.*

- Celli, B.R., MacNee, W., & ATS/ERS Task Force. (2004). *Standards for the diagnosis and treatment of patients with COPD: a summary of the ATS/ERS position paper. European Respiratory Journal.*

- Cooper, C.B., & Barjaktarevic, I. (2019). *A new algorithm for the management of COPD. Chest.*

- Diaz-Guzman, E., & Mannino, D.M. (2014). *Epidemiology and prevalence of chronic obstructive pulmonary disease. Clinics in Chest Medicine.*

- Global Initiative for Chronic Obstructive Lung Disease (GOLD). (2020). *Global strategy for the diagnosis, management, and prevention of COPD. GOLD Report.*

- Hogg, J.C. (2004). *Pathophysiology of airflow limitation in chronic obstructive pulmonary disease. Lancet.*

- Holguin, F., Folch, E., Redd, S.C., & Mannino, D.M. (2005). *Comorbidity and mortality in COPD-related hospitalizations in the United States, 1979 to 2001. Chest, 128(4).*

- Miravitlles, M., Anzueto, A., & Blasi, F. (2017). *Prevention of exacerbations in chronic obstructive pulmonary disease: knowns and unknowns. Chronic Respiratory Disease.*

- Nici, L., & ZuWallack, R. (2012). *Pulmonary rehabilitation for chronic obstructive pulmonary disease. New England Journal of Medicine.*

- Rabe, K.F., Watz, H. (2017). *Chronic obstructive pulmonary disease. Lancet.*

www.ingramcontent.com/pod-product-compliance
Lightning Source LLC
Chambersburg PA
CBHW060919130726
48001CB00006B/2312